A Mindset to Success

———— *By* ————

Kayleigh Greenacre

Copyright © 2021 Kayleigh Greenacre

All rights reserved.

No part of this publication may be reproduced, distributed or transmitted in any form or by any means, including photocopying, recording or other electronic or mechanical methods, without the prior written permission of the publisher, except in the case of brief quotations, reviews and other noncommercial uses permitted by copyright law.

First published and distributed in the United Kingdom by: Amazon.co.uk

This book is dedicated to my beautiful daughter Sofia Grace. You are my biggest inspiration and the reason why this book exists today - to empower and inspire all the amazing females out there who deserve to reach their dreams!

A SPECIAL THANK YOU AND ACKNOWLEDGEMENTS

To everyone who has supported me through my journey of developing my career and business as well as growing as an individual - thank you. My mum and dad for your years of guidance and advice; my brother Tarren for your many words of wisdom; and all my close friends and loved ones. Thank you for your ongoing support and encouragement as well as believing in me, making this a reality.

WHO ARE YOU?

You are positive and determined.

You have self-belief, courage and confidence.

You have clear goals and aims you wish to accomplish.

You accept failure as part of learning and developing.

You CAN change your limiting beliefs into new empowered ones!

You understand that not everything is easy and some things take time.

You have a growth mindset.

You create your own happiness and success by believing in yourself.

You follow your excitement, passion and enthusiasm and allow your dreams to come true.

You are UNSTOPPABLE!

You believe that **'Actually...I Can!'** achieve anything you set your mind to.

CONTENTS

A special thank you and Acknowledgements v
Who are you? vii
Introduction 1
Chapter 1. Your Purpose 3
Chapter 2. Goals and Dreams 9
Chapter 3. Luck, Fate and Gratitude 22
Chapter 4. I Give Up … I'm a Failure. My limiting beliefs 32
Chapter 5. Your Mindset 43
Chapter 6. Motivation 58
Chapter 7. The Language We Use 69
Chapter 8. Visualisation 76
Chapter 9. Reflections 83
Chapter 10. The Future 87
About the Author 91
Stay Connected and get Involved 93

INTRODUCTION

*I*f you were given two options in life: to stay as you are today for the rest of your life, or to continue believing, growing and achieving, what would you choose?

Our lives today are so busy and complex that many people find it hard to stay positive. Juggling work, housework and chores, children, relationships, social lives, hobbies and interests, as well as dealing with health challenges, financial concerns and fear, we all find, at some point, that life is a struggle. These struggles and challenges can encourage people to be negative and develop a fixed mindset. A fixed mindset is where the individual's mind is static and does not accept that it can develop or grow.

The way we train our brains to think has a huge impact on our lives. We create our own success and happiness. If we have a growth mindset and self-belief, we can approach life's challenges with a positive outlook, believing that we can achieve whatever we aim for. If you have optimism, gratitude, the ability to accept failure, resilience and self-belief you WILL be successful.

Success is possible for everyone and your goals and dreams are achievable … as long as you have the right mindset.

Use this book to support you with your mindset and your goals which you desire to achieve because you are capable of achieving success.

CHAPTER 1

Your Purpose

We all have a purpose in life, and that is to live the best life we can, to reach our full potential and fulfil our inner happiness. Our purpose can often be obscured by our worries and our insecurities, which can sometimes make us question our purpose. However, we should all be focusing on enjoying our lives and ensuring that we combine our passions with our aims and goals to develop a growth mindset, to grow as a person and to create our own happiness.

Some people believe that they have a sole purpose, something they need to fulfil within their lifetime, but this purpose isn't always easy to figure out. One of the most common questions we are asked when we are young is 'What do you want to be when you are older?' Many children have absolutely no answer to this question, which leaves them feeling empty, uncertain and confused. Sometimes it takes people many years to work out their purpose and what they need to do to give their life meaning.

We are often guided down a 'safe' path by our parents, teachers and employers – such as accepting a job that they see as being suitable or considering the cost of university and whether we will benefit from it – but what if this safe path isn't the path we are meant to go down to fulfil our full potential in life? Sometimes we need to take risks and to be open to options that are not as 'safe' as others, to find out more about ourselves and discover what we are really good at. Over time, our purpose becomes more clear: we realise what we want to achieve, what we are aiming for and how we can achieve it.

Having a sense of purpose helps us to think about what we want to achieve. It also makes us feel happier about ourselves and our lives because we wake up in the morning knowing what we are working towards and where we are going, feeling energised, focused and satisfied, knowing that the outcome or reward will be worth achieving.

This can be related to *ikigai*, a Japanese term that translates as 'a reason to live'. A number of things can be defined as *ikigai*: what we love and enjoy the most in life; what we are really good at doing; how we can contribute to other people's lives and the world itself; the things we receive rewards for, such as an income from our job.

What we love and enjoy in life: We should focus on what makes us smile, or those activities that make us feel warm and fulfilled, that take away emptiness, doubt or loneliness. This could be something as simple as watching a chick flick in your PJs on a Sunday afternoon or meeting up with your friends to socialise.

I have a number of things that make me smile: I love to teach females about growth mindset and how to grow their businesses; to play the saxophone or piano when I need some escapism; to take photos and videos; to watch inspirational films; to spend time with my friends and family; to focus on my own growth and self-development. Each of us has our own interests and hobbies in life which make us motivated and happy: these are what helps us to understand our purpose.

What we are really good at doing: What skills do you have? This could be anything, such as academic writing, cooking or baking, craft-making, running long distances, playing hockey, playing a musical instrument, or just simply supporting your family and friends. We use our skills regularly in our lives to make us happy or to fulfil our needs or other people's needs. This can be both at, and outside of work. People develop new skills throughout their life. This demonstrates our ability to continue learning and improving something to achieve the best outcome. Examples of this include: a baby learning to walk; a child learning to read or write; a teenager learning to play football; an adult learning to drive. The new skills we learn can be ones we choose to learn or ones we naturally develop over time. Continuing to develop our skills in life will make us feel more fulfilled and will contribute towards our sense of purpose and achievement.

How we can contribute to other people's lives and the world itself: What do you do to support others and make them happy, or for the good of our world? This could be anything from doing favours for friends or family members, such as helping them repair a broken-down car or doing a food shop for them when they are poorly. This could also be supporting the wider society by doing things to help make our world a better, healthier place for future generations, such as recycling, supporting charities or minimising our carbon footprint. Often when we offer other people our help, support, skills or knowledge, we feel satisfied and happy. We get a sense of fulfilment from supporting other people and making them happy. Some people even find that giving to others is more rewarding than receiving things themselves.

The things we receive rewards for: What do we get paid for or receive a reward for? The income we receive for doing our job is one of the most obvious here, but are there many other ways in which we are rewarded for what we achieve or complete. Gratitude and a 'thank you' from someone is a kind of reward – a sign of thanks for something positive that you have done in someone else's life.

Most of us follow a linear pathway leading to success with a reward at the end: we seek validation from other people that we have accomplished our goal or aim – for example, through a pay rise or a promotion. Most people will work harder if they know they will receive a reward at the end of it. An example of this is a bonus scheme at work: the more revenue an individual brings into the company from leads and sales, the bigger the bonus the individual will receive. We are, more often than not, motivated by reward, regardless of whether this is related to money or something else, such as kudos or gratitude.

I used Ikigai years ago to find my purpose. Although I knew I wanted to be successful and to be happy with my achievements, I wasn't 100% certain what that looked like and what my life purpose actually was. I therefore started to look into the four main areas of Ikigai which was a starting point for discovering my purpose. I started to think about and write down the things I love (work, socialising, growth mindset, music, teaching others, photography and videography). I then looked at what I am good at. Many of my answers seemed to link to what I like (communication, teaching, supporting others, coaching, mentoring, performing, music, photography). I then looked at what the world needs specifically from me (my motivation and skills to inspire others to believe in themselves so that they too can be successful), and then the rewards to receive from this (gratitude, recognition and development). By looking at my answers I could then make connections between each of the areas which helped me to identify ways of achieving balance within the areas and to identify 'my purpose': inspiring, coaching and teaching others to believe in themselves in order to achieve their goals. This clarified my happiness and fulfilment and developed my own career success through really focusing on Ikigai and creating my purpose.

Your purpose can change when elements in your life change: for example, if you change jobs, your feelings will change towards your career and your previous job. You may well question your purpose, or you may have a renewed sense of enthusiasm. Life is a constant process of self-discovery: what do you wish to achieve? Taking small steps to achieve each goal will keep you feeling positive and will ultimately help you to achieve your goals.

Now it's your turn

Use a journal to complete the tasks throughout this book.

Think about the questions below and answer them in your reflection journal as best you can. If you look again at these questions in six months, or in a year, after reading this book and working through the exercises, your answers may well have changed.

- Who am I?
- What do I have to contribute to the world? (Consider your job, lifestyle, family and friends, etc.)
- What are my core beliefs, morals and principles?
- Write down the four *ikigai* principles – what you love and enjoy the most in your life; what you are really good at doing; how you can contribute to other people's lives and the world itself; the things you receive rewards for. Then make a list of each one that applies to you. So, underneath 'what you are really good at doing', you might add 'cooking, baking, photography, listening to people'.

Be a girl with confidence, a woman with courage and a lady with self-belief.

CHAPTER 2

Goals and Dreams

We all dream of achieving something, whether it is something small and tangible or something big and imaginative. Some of us dream of being the CEO of a successful company, whereas others dream of falling in love with the perfect partner. Dreams have a way of connecting our inner thoughts with our imagination. They raise our level of excitement, making us feel positive about the possible outcomes. They can make the impossible seem possible and can positively impact how we view various situations and opportunities. Dreams can help us to process our emotions and motivate us to achieve. We are always told to dream big – that achieving whatever we wish to achieve is possible, and that there are no limitations to achieving that dream.

It doesn't matter how far you currently are from achieving that dream; if someone else is doing it, then you can too. Children always have the most imaginative dreams, with no limitations: they want to become an astronaut, a doctor, a football player, or a prince or princess with a fire-breathing dragon as a pet. These dreams may stem from interests in careers, topics, cultures, media and history and create no barriers to their imagination because as children we are allowed to be imaginative, encouraged to be creative and have freedom to be whoever we want to be.

When I was a young child, I was such a confident soul - always happy and keen to learn and try new things. I felt consistently energised and excited with the thought of a new adventure or opportunity. I had an ultimate dream and goal of becoming famous by performing on stage, and to be honest with you – I believed I could make it! There was nothing that was going to stop me because I was convinced that that is what I wanted to achieve. I had no doubt and no fears as a child in relation to what I wanted to be, I just knew that that is what I wanted to achieve.

As we grow older, we continue to dream of what we may want to achieve; however, many of us become more conscious of our fears, worries and limiting beliefs and start to feel that our dreams are not achievable because we subconsciously create barriers for ourselves ('Oh, I'll never be able to get that promotion, I'm too inexperienced and not confident enough). We may find ourselves dreaming of things that seem perfect yet are so far away from what we currently have, and therefore we are quick to shut down the possibility of it becoming true or real. As individuals, we are in control of our dreams, our thoughts, and what is actually achievable in our lives, because it is down to our self-belief and mindset as to what we can achieve.

However, a dream on its own is just a thought – it isn't real. Dreams are dictated by the power of your imagination. A dream, in fact, is a desire, wish or fantasy that is created in our mind: for example, we might dream of becoming a multi 6 figure business owner. These dreams do not have a timeframe or a real focus; they are subjective rather than objective. If you turn these dreams into objective goals or aims, with clear, achievable targets and steps as to how you can reach your end goal and, potentially, your dream, then you can turn your dreams into reality. The goals and aims you set yourself need to be realistic and achievable. If you dream of owning a unicorn or having a money tree, this just won't happen because these things don't actually exist. However, if you set yourself achievable goals and aims – no matter how hard it may seem to achieve them and how far from them you are – the majority of dreams are possible, providing you have the resources and physical / mental ability.

Imagine that your dream is to become a famous actress and star in a blockbuster film. Now, for most people this would seem impossible to achieve, but this *could* be achievable if you create a plan with small targets to achieve. For example, to start this journey you could attend stage school or acting classes; without acting skills and the opportunity to develop as an actress, you wouldn't normally be able to star in a blockbuster film. Once you were attending classes, you could set yourself a new goal of performing in a local performance or play. By setting small, realistic goals, over time you will make progress and – hopefully – get closer to your end goal of being able to star in a blockbuster film.

Everyone has life goals and aims, whether this is 'to be happy and loved by the people around me' or 'to earn a six-figure salary'. Whatever your goal is, you can achieve it if you stay positive and have a growth mindset – and a clear plan of how you can achieve it.

What's the difference between dreams and goals?

Dreams	**Goals**
Require imagination	Require hard work
Inspire you as a person	Can change your life
Produce imaginary results	Produce tangible results

Are something you think about	Are things you can action
Are generally more abstract	Are more measurable and specific
Don't have a timescale or ending	Have an end point and a timeframe

This demonstrates that a dream on its own won't produce the results you want in real life. Instead, you need to work with your dreams to set yourself a goal – something that is specific and measurable, that can be regularly reviewed and adapted, if necessary, to make the end result achievable. A goal gives people a visual end result, which motivates people to work towards that end result. If you set clear, measurable goals, you can easily monitor the progress you are making – and celebrate when you achieve each stage of your goal.

Many people believe in the 'Law of Attraction', which encourages individuals to focus on what they really want (their goal or aim), to visualise it, then to take action towards achieving it – which will, hopefully, eventually end with the result they want. The idea is, that if you focus your mind on what you want to manifest and you unlock the power of your subconscious mind, you can attract positive energy and bring love, health, freedom and happiness into your life. This idea links to a positive mindset or a growth mindset: if you focus on what you want to achieve, and believe you can achieve it, then you stand a better chance of achieving it.

We start setting ourselves goals at a very young age. Babies develop so quickly during their first year that they seem to be learning new things every day. Although babies are too young to understand the concept of goals, parents may set goals for their babies and help them to achieve these goals, such as sitting up, walking, talking and feeding themselves, then celebrate the success of accomplishing these. Babies are at the very early stages of development, both mentally and physically. They know what they want, but they need to work out how they can reach that goal. For example, if a six-month-old sees a toy on the other side of the room that they want to play with, they need to work out how to get to that toy. This could be done by learning to crawl, bum-shuffling, or finding another way of moving themselves across the floor towards the toy before they are able to walk. These skills come with time. A few years down the line, toddlers and young children will set themselves goals (with the help of their parents/guardians), such as tying their shoelaces, putting on their own clothes and going to the toilet on their own. These small, everyday actions help young children to become more independent over time, and are important in preparation for starting school.

As we grow older, our goals and aims become slightly more complex, involving many more people, steps and barriers to overcome. Teenagers set themselves goals: to pass their GCSEs and A-levels and leave school to start a career or go to college or university. In fact, the school years can be seen as the most challenging. Students take a number of subjects, learning different topics and skills within each, from learning how to apply theories in maths to understanding the complexities of the English language. Teenagers face many challenges at school that test their ability to build resilience and believe in themselves. Teachers, careers advisors and support staff in schools often help students to set goals and targets to support their knowledge and understanding of a subject as well as their progress over time; however it is down to the individual student to believe in these goals and aims and put in the work to achieve them.

If you do not believe that something is achievable, it will be much harder to achieve, thus your understanding of each goal and aim is extremely important. I have set students and clients targets, goals and aims over my years of being an education practitioner and a mindset / business coach; however, I have found that if the student or client does not actually understand the goal/target and how to achieve it, it is very unlikely that they will ever achieve it.

After we leave school, we normally start on a career path and will set ourselves new goals and aims. Some people choose to go to university to study for a degree in a subject that will help them to pursue their career goals (such as studying medicine to become a doctor), while others will prefer to start work to learn a trade or skills that they can develop over time so they become more successful in their chosen area. Both pathways create opportunities for individuals to believe in, develop and achieve their goals. One of the goals I set myself at university was to attend all lectures and seminars every day and to visit the university library at least once a week to keep up with the set reading for my course. Although my attendance was extremely good throughout my time at school and university, I had little interest in reading and had no ambition to read books relating to my course, as this just didn't interest me at the time. However, we had to read the journals, books and articles on the set reading list to pass the course, therefore this was something I had to complete. I therefore ensured that I attended the library every Monday afternoon to read the literature for that week. This was a realistic, achievable goal. It was also beneficial, as it supported my knowledge and understanding of the topics we covered each week. Years later, I now love reading non-fiction books, articles and journals on topics that interest me, as I generally learn so much from them. This fuels my enthusiasm for the topic or fills in any gaps in my knowledge and understanding. Throughout my time at university and when I was starting my career, I set myself many goals to help myself focus on what I wanted to achieve, who I wanted to become, and how I wanted to develop.

Regardless of the route we choose to take, we all have dreams and goals. They do not have to be career-related; they can be anything we aspire to achieve in adulthood.

When you are setting goals, you need to think hard about what you want to achieve. What do your goals look like? What are you passionate about and what is your vision? This will vary from person to person, depending on their current life stage and how much they want to challenge themselves to achieve their goal. Goals should be realistic and achievable, but can be as challenging and aspirational as you want. There is no right or wrong way of setting goals in your life or career, but I have set out four steps below, which contain some tips that you may find useful.

How to set a goal for yourself

Step 1

Think about what you really want from life. Think about the top five things you want to achieve. Imagine yourself actually achieving these and the effect it would have on you and your life. You could consider actions like graduating from university, starting your own business, buying your first house, starting a family.

Here are some areas to think about when considering what goals you'd like to set:

- Attitude – your mindset and how you view life.
- Business / Career – your future goal for your current business or career, or even a new area.
- Education – knowledge and understanding of a subject that you wish to develop over time.
- Family – from expanding your family to supporting others in your family.
- Financial – the money you wish to earn (through your career, a business idea or other ways).
- Physical – a goal linked to your physical self, such as strength, stamina or body shape.

Choose goals and aims that will challenge you and that you can work towards over time. Do they have the potential to change your life in a positive way? Are they bigger and better than what you currently have? Will they make you happy? Also ensure that your goals are SMART:

S – Specific

M – Measurable

A – Achievable

R – Realistic

T – Timely

Setting SMART goals gives you a clear idea of what you want to achieve and helps you focus on this. It will also motivate you to achieve your specific target. It clarifies your goal and encourages you to evaluate your achievement after a certain time.

For example:

Specific: To create my own business that I can run from home.

Measurable: To have at least 100 orders in the first six months. To monitor sales over the first few months.

Achievable: By promoting my business and products on social media and by word of mouth, I will be able to achieve this, if I am persistent.

Relevant: If I'm successful, this will lead to more sales and reaching a wider audience – and therefore create more profit.

Time-bound: After six months, I will have achieved 100 sales.

Step 2

Once you know the main goal or goals you want to achieve, start to break these down into smaller targets or steps you can take to start achieving the goal. Consider the timeframe for each small target and have a clear plan of what you want to achieve by when. An example of this could look like the following:

Goal 1 – To create my own business that I can run from home.

Time	*Steps*	*What is involved*
Week 1	Research into my chosen products or services to sell and work out my 'why'.	Market research asking my potential dream clients what they would want support with. Writing down my target audience, the support I can give, the results I can create and working out the overall 'why'.
Weeks 2–4	Develop a business plan for my new business considering: branding, messaging, marketing, sales, resources, logistics etc…	Using a business plan template to support me with creating a business plan. Further market research will be needed.

Weeks 5–12	Start planning my products and services and how they will be available to audiences.	Start designing the products themselves and create the finished products for audiences.
Week 13	Marketing and sales	Consider and create engaging content to support with marketing and selling the products.

Step 3

When you start working towards your targets, be sure to evaluate the progress you are making. Adapt when necessary if things are not working out the way they should or are not getting you closer to your end goal. One way to do this is to use a reflection journal or notebook to reflect on the progress you are making and keep a record of your progress. You could do this on a regular basis – daily, weekly or monthly. For example:

Monday 23 June

Today I worked with my business coach to gain an insight into marketing for a business and the most effective ways of doing this. She showed me a range of marketing strategies that she has used in the last year for her own business, both online (e.g. social media platforms, website) and offline (e.g. print advertising). This has increased my knowledge of marketing techniques and strategies that I could apply to my own business. I now feel I have a better knowledge and

> *understanding of marketing techniques to support business growth.*
>
> *My next step will be to research a range of other marketing strategies that have been used in my industry sector and compare what those strategies consist of, including tools, content and designs.*

Step 4

Believe in yourself. Believe that any goal you set yourself is achievable. The power of self-belief is huge, and can be the motivation you need to achieve your goal or aim and to make your dream come true. If you don't believe in yourself, then how can you expect others to believe in you?

Search out opportunities that will help with your personal growth. Some opportunities may not give the results you intended, but if you believe in yourself and continue to follow your goals, aims and vision, better results will follow.

When you start working towards your goals, it is important that you stay focused and don't let any hurdles demotivate you or hold you back. There will always be hurdles along the way and achieving your goal may not always be plain sailing. However, having a growth mindset and focusing on the end goal will motivate you to keep going, striving and progressing.

Whatever goals you set yourself and the steps you wish to take to achieve these, make sure you write them down. Thinking of what you want to achieve and setting yourself goals in your mind is one thing, but actually writing them down, creating a plan and actually regularly evaluating them will encourage you to manifest them faster. When you write them down and regularly revisit them, you are reaffirming in your mind what you want to achieve and how you intend to achieve it. I was once told by one of my friends that if you write your dreams and goals down and actually put them onto paper, they then exist in a physical form and are now not just a thought in your mind.

I started writing down my goals in my mid-twenties, thinking about what I wanted to achieve before I was 30. I regularly revisited my goals and I also had a reminder of these at work in my office to remind me every single day of what I wanted to achieve. I set myself small steps of how to achieve these and worked for them throughout my twenties. Although I didn't tick every goal off my list by the time I was 30, the majority of them I did achieve because I believed in my dreams and goals and knew what I had to do to achieve them by having a clear plan in place and reflecting and reviewing the process.

Now it's your turn

In your reflection journal, write down your dream – the one thing you really wish for. Look at this dream and see if it is achievable (be realistic) and if it can be turned into a goal or a set of mini-goals. Write out these goals, ensuring they are SMART. Create a plan for how you will achieve these goals, and over what timeframe. Ensure you reflect on every step of the way in your reflection journal. Reflecting on your thoughts, processes and progress will encourage you to evaluate what is effective and what isn't.

Little girls with dreams become women with a goal & a vision.

CHAPTER 3

Luck, Fate and Gratitude

*E*veryone has good days and bad days. Many things happen in our lives that we are unable to control, and these can affect our thoughts and feelings towards certain people and situations. It's not always easy to remain positive – we all feel pessimistic at times. But how we react to and learn from these situations is important. It will help us to develop a stronger growth mindset.

Many psychologists have explored the idea of a growth mindset and positivity. Some believe that having to face challenges helps with personal growth. This means that you treat challenges of your life as a learning opportunity, enabling you to devise a way to overcome the problem, negative thought or barrier. A negative thought is a thought, often recurring, that makes you feel bad, such as thinking that a goal isn't achievable or thinking about all the worst things that could happen in a given situation.

If you were asked to make a list of all the negative things that have happened to you over the last week or all the challenges that you have faced, what would be on your list? Were you able to overcome these? How manageable were they? Were some of them controllable, and did you learn anything from any of them?

In the past, I have experienced streaks of 'bad luck'. One year, everything seemed to go wrong. No matter what I did or how much I pitied myself, I was unable to change it, and negative things kept happening to me. I genuinely thought it was 'just my luck' and I struggled to change my mindset, to believe that I was lucky in other aspects of life, and that positive things were also happening to me all the time. I chose to focus on the negative aspects and was unable to see past these. I often questioned why these things were happening to me and why I was so unlucky in comparison to my friends and other people around me. Little did I know at the time, but it was all to do with my mindset and how I reacted to situations that could either be seen as 'unlucky' or as lessons to learn from.

Many people believe in 'luck' – after all, it's all down to luck if you win the lottery or find your perfect partner. But is luck a myth, or does it actually exist? In my early twenties, I always used to wonder why some people I knew seemed to be much luckier than me in regards to success, money etc. 'What do they do that I don't?' I looked at successful famous people and wondered if they were born lucky or if there was a secret to their success. But what if 'luck' isn't a gift that's given to certain people but instead an outcome linked to mindset? If we believe ourselves to be unlucky, then the outcome may be just that. However, if we change our mindset to think that we are lucky or that good luck is on its way, then our outcomes tend to be far more positive. This links to how positive thinking and a growth mindset can make you more lucky because your positivity affects how you see life and opportunities that come your way.

When we feel lucky, or we go through what I call a 'lucky streak', we feel happy and positive, but sometimes we may start to question *why* we are currently so lucky and when our luck is going to run out. If you believe in luck, you believe that someone is giving you good luck and that this can easily be taken away. This makes us feel powerless: that what happens in our life is not down to our hard work but is all down to chance. You can relate this to rolling a dice. Say you want to roll a 6. The probability of you rolling a 6 is one in six. If you are 'lucky', you could roll a 6. Another example is the weather on your wedding day. Everyone wants their wedding day to be perfect and sunny with no rain. The chances of it raining depends on the location, the season/month and the general weather forecast for that day, but if you are 'lucky' it won't rain. Therefore, is believing in luck taking away our power to being able to control and create our own outcomes?

Luck also links to fate; many people believe in fate, that things happen for a reason, and what is meant to be will be. We are all individuals with unique pathways through life. Fate is the concept that we have to play the cards we have been dealt; we cannot change them. Some people are born into wealthy families and others are not; some people face many challenges throughout their childhood, and others will not. Although many individuals believe that this is true, we are able to intervene with fate and the stages planned out for us in our lives to change what could be into something completely different. Some people believe that through a combination of luck and fate, they have no way to change things that happen to them. They feel that they are unlucky and will never be successful. However, this is not true, this is a negative mindset. We are in control of our own lives and futures. No matter how 'lucky' or 'unlucky' you think you are, you stand a better chance of achieving what you desire or aim for if you change your mindset. You should focus on what you want to achieve and really work for it as your goals are achievable regardless of your background.

Gratitude

If we shift our mindset of luck and fate to gratitude, how would this change things? Gratitude means appreciating and being thankful for what we have or for things that have happened to us. It's all about perception – how we see things. We should be able to be grateful and thankful for everything in our lives. Some people would argue that this can't possibly apply to negative things that happen to us, such as being made redundant or being a victim of crime. However, what if we think about what these negative situations led to and how they changed other aspects of our lives? Showing gratitude is an effective way of making us feel positive about anything in our lives. It's good to think hard about what we are grateful for. We should practise being grateful for even the simplest things – such as being healthy, having a roof over our heads and having food to eat each day – because, after all, there are many people in the world who do not have these things. Are you guilty of taking these for granted? When did you last stop and think about what you are grateful for? Our lives are often so busy that we miss opportunities to be grateful for what we have. It is easy to feel sorry for ourselves when things do not go our way. However, being grateful more regularly has many benefits. Some of these benefits are listed below:

- It makes us happier, and encourages us to feel more positive and optimistic.
- It develops our self-esteem to make us feel more confident.
- It develops our self-belief.
- It strengthens our emotions, making us feel positive, stronger and happier.

- It makes us more sociable and more likeable attracting people to us because of our positive mindset.
- It encourages success by making us more positive, driven and focused.

Does looking at these potential benefits encourage you to apply gratitude more regularly in your life? If being grateful helps us to be mentally stronger or make us happier and more positive, then why wouldn't we do it?

I discovered that you become a happier person when you show gratitude. When I was first setting up my business 'Actually, I Can!' I was stressed with trying to juggle my full-time job, being a mum, having a social life as well as starting my own business. I couldn't seem to find the time to fit everything in and although I had set myself my goals, I couldn't see how I was actually going to achieve them as they seemed so far away. I then remembered that my mindset really impacts how I feel, my motivation and also my achievements. I then changed my perspective; I remained focused and thought daily about what I was most grateful for. This gave me the opportunity to really think about gratitude and encouraged me to remain positive throughout the stressful times.

Practising gratitude regularly can avoid hedonic adaptation (a theory that states people always return to their original level of happiness, regardless of what events take place in their lives or what happens to them). Gratitude keeps us happier for longer without us falling back into our usual state of mind and thinking negative thoughts. Hedonic adaptation states that if something good happens to a person (such as winning the lottery) intense feelings of happiness and positivity soon die off and your mind returns to its 'normal' state. This also happens with life events such as getting married, moving into a bigger house or receiving a promotion at work. Over time, your mind will return to its original state of happiness as the novelty of the new event gradually wears off.

Negative events can have a massive impact on people and their confidence, self-esteem and mood. I have learned, that although negative things happen to me, and some of those things happen because of other people's greed and anger, I have gradually started to appreciate, and be thankful for the good things in my life, such as my beautiful daughter, a lovely family home and a secure and rewarding job. When we experience negative events it feels very unpleasant and can make us feel upset, emotional and angry. However, when you are able to overcome the shock of the negative event, you are then able to feel grateful for what you currently have and relieved that you are healthy and safe.

An effective way of being able to identify what you are grateful for is by starting every morning thinking of three things that you are grateful for in your life – it's a great way to start the day and an exercise that I implement regularly. Gratitude is a powerful tool that makes you appreciate what you have and moves you away from thinking you are 'lucky' or 'unlucky'.

There are many ways that we can show gratitude for what we have in our lives and show gratitude to others. Here are a few, which are simple and effective:

1. **Be present.** It's amazing how powerful your presence can be to people. Simply turning up to an event to support a friend or family member can show them that you are there for them and that you are grateful to have them in your life. Your presence can help make people feel valued and loved.
2. **Say thank you.** One of the easiest ways of showing gratitude is to say thank you to either yourself or someone else for giving/providing you with something. This can

be something as small as saying 'thank you' to a driver who stops at a crossing to let you cross the road. The words 'thank you' should be easy to say, and are generally appreciated by people.

3. **Smile.** Show others and yourself that you are happy and grateful for the things around you. Often, when you see a person smiling you can see that they are genuinely happy. If you smile at others, it shows them that you are grateful to be in their company and happy to see them.

4. **Give compliments.** This has a positive impact on people's self-esteem and can make someone feel more confident and happy, so show your gratitude by complimenting someone on their new top or hairstyle or a great piece of work they have done. Simply saying to someone, 'You've done a great job on that project – well done!' can boost their confidence and self-esteem. It also shows them that you are grateful for what they have done.

5. **Commit acts of kindness.** This means doing something for someone who may need your help – for example, buying some food for a homeless person or contributing to a food bank. This shows that you are grateful that you can buy food for yourself, and the recipient will no doubt be grateful for your generosity. There are many 'acts of kindness' that you can do which will be gratefully received, no matter how small or simple they are.

6. **Share your talents.** If you have a specific skill or talent, share it with others who may need it or who could benefit from it. An example of this could be sharing your top business tips with your social media audience, with your friends or sharing tips for the latest fashion trends. This will demonstrate that you are grateful for having this knowledge or skill, and wish to help others by sharing your knowledge with them.

7. **Have the courage to share your thoughts with other people.** It takes courage to open up and discuss your health and happiness. Talking openly about your experiences and why you are so happy in certain areas of your life, shows that you are grateful for what you have received or achieved. This can have a positive effect on others and can help them to develop courage for themselves.
8. **Provide encouragement.** Encourage others to work towards their goals and dreams by offering advice or kind, inspiring words and by appreciating your progress towards your own goals. Reflecting on your own achievements and offering support to others from what you have learned is an effective way of showing gratitude to others.
9. **Grow.** Be grateful for what you already have, but try to better yourself even further by formulating strategies to really 'grow' as a person. Consider how you have grown over the past months and years, and think about what you are grateful for that has supported you to do this. For example, be honest to others and yourself. Don't make excuses for mistakes you have made, and discover new things that interest you.
10. **Keep a gratitude journal.** Start to keep a journal, where you can reflect every day on what you are grateful for. Reflecting on what you have, and what you have achieved, is a fantastic way of acknowledging your gratitude for everything in your life. These can be accomplishments or they can be the simplest things in life: for example, memorable times with your family, a job promotion, the house you have just bought

The final point is a very effective strategy for improving your growth mindset. It encourages you to stop and think about what you are grateful for. Having a written gratitude journal will clearly show this, and it's interesting to look back at it and see what you listed six months ago or a year ago. It's also a good way of reflecting on your current state of mind and the positives in your life.

The best way to do this is:

1. Find a time when you can sit and think, with no distractions.
2. Think about all the things in your life that you are grateful for. This could be something as simple as 'I am grateful that I have a roof over my head, that I am healthy and that I have a loving family.'
3. Repeat this exercise every day, and see the positive impact it has on your mindset.</>

Now it's your turn

- Write down the five negative things that have happened in your life or challenges that you have had to face.
- Were you able to overcome these and move on from them? If so, write down how you did this.
- Now start a gratitude journal. You can use your reflection journal for this. For thirty days, write down each day what you are grateful for, and see how doing this changes your mindset. Try to consider all areas of your life – work, home, family, friends, hobbies, health.
- In your gratitude journal, also make a note of how you have shown gratitude for the good things in your life. (Some of these could be the strategies discussed in this chapter.)

Show gratitude for what you have today and see how this builds on your 'tomorrow'.

CHAPTER 4

I Give Up ... I'm a Failure. My limiting beliefs.

Have you ever not been offered a job you applied for or not achieved the GCSE/A-level grades you expected to get into university? Have you ever lost at a sports game? Have you ever attempted to create something, which didn't turn out the way you had hoped? Have you got divorced or has your marriage broken down? Have you ever felt like a failure? But what does 'failure' mean? Does it mean not achieving your intended outcome – or is it a lesson to learn from, which encourages you to accept that things don't always work out straight away and that you can learn and grow from the situation?

Everyone fails at things in life, but what can we learn from our failures? Many people believe that 'failing' is attempting something and not achieving it. However, why should we accept our first attempt as the only attempt? A great example of this is taking your driving test. Some people pass first time and others pass on their third, fourth or fifth attempt. If you failed your driving test the first time, would you never take it again? People take their driving test so they can travel from place to place. Therefore, people usually choose to retake their driving test if they fail, because being able to drive will make it easier for them to get to work, school and to get around. So surely this concept can be applied to everything? Many people even use failure as a step towards success or achieving something.

The key here is to understand that even if you fail at something the first, second or even third time you try it, persistence and determination will help you to focus on your end goal and help you achieve it. Athletes are a great example of this. Footballers, gymnasts, basketball players and many others will all have experienced failure – losing a race or a match, failing to master a skill within their sport. By them using a growth mindset, they are able to channel their mind and focus on their aim. Imagine being asked to do twenty keepie-uppies with a football – but you have never tried doing them before. The likelihood is that you will not be able to do twenty the first time round. If you had failed to do twenty keepie-uppies, you'd probably want to give it another go to see if you improve. Naturally over time, your ability to do these would develop through practice and perseverance. This applies to everything in life: practice makes perfect.

The same is true for making mistakes. We all make mistakes in life. Sometimes these can cause setbacks and barriers to achieving what we want. We can all learn from our mistakes by understanding why things went wrong. Mistakes can create challenges and obstacles, all of which you can overcome if you set your mind to it. When you give in to negativity and pessimism, you will naturally feel unhappy and therefore will push away opportunities for growth and success. Many of us fear failing, we doubt ourselves at times and worry about the implications of making a mistake or failing at something. Many of us shy away from challenges and can become disheartened when we make mistakes. However, making a mistake actually creates an opportunity for someone to learn from it, to grow and improve their skills, knowledge and competencies. If things were always easy and people remained in their comfort zone, they would not progress. We should be inspired by challenge and difficulty to better ourselves.

Many students are afraid of making mistakes in class, such as failing to solve a GCSE algebra equation. They don't want people to think they're stupid or incapable. Why should mistakes be seen as negative? Why do people want to avoid making mistakes? If students are told from a young age that making mistakes is totally normal, accepted and expected, then they should feel more able to take on new challenges that will develop their skills and abilities within that subject area. If students are confident about offering an answer in class, risking that it might be wrong, they will quickly learn from their mistakes and be able to focus on how to reach the right answer. This applies to almost everything in life: where mistakes can be made, there are lessons to be learned and progress to be made. Accepting their mistakes can make people mentally stronger and more resilient, therefore more likely to achieve their end goal.

I have made many mistakes in my life, from failing my driving test, to saying things I shouldn't to people I care about. I have also felt in the past that I have failed as a mother by not being able to spend as much quality time with my daughter as many other mothers do, due to my career and taking on too much at work not considering the impact it would have on my home life. However, I have learnt from this that by managing my time carefully and ensuring I have that quality time with my daughter each day after she finishes school,

I am then able to balance and juggle both my career and being a mummy.

We all make mistakes. The main point I want to make here is that we should all use our mistakes as opportunities to learn and move forward. It is important that we see the value of our mistakes and not dwell on the negatives, as this will affect our performance and self-confidence. Sometimes we even try to blame other people or make excuses for our mistakes, to cover the fact that we made a mistake in the first place. The mistakes we make happen for a reason. They alert us to the fact that we are on the wrong path to our intended final outcome, thus allowing us to change track. A mistake can be seen as a 'signpost' that shows you where you need to go. If you choose to ignore a 'signpost' and continue along the same path, you may be delayed or side-tracked from your goal, and it will take you longer to reach it.

Mistakes also inform us that there is room for improvement. This gives us something to aim for, motivating us to keep going and working towards our end goal. Let's apply this theory to a real-life situation: baking a Victoria sponge. There are many things that bakers can get wrong here: choosing the wrong ingredients, making a mistake in weighing the ingredients, using the wrong method to mix the batter, setting the oven at the wrong temperature, leaving the cake in the oven too long, and so on. If you make a Victoria sponge and bake the cake for too long, it will result in a hard, dry sponge. If you reflect on your methods you will find out that there is room for improvement: you could check more regularly on the cake's progress in the oven or set a timer to ensure you don't over-bake the cake. Although this is a simple example, this way of identifying mistakes and working out how to improve them can be applied to almost any situation.

Risk Taking

Risk-taking is also another factor to consider. If you take risks, you are challenging yourself. However, these risks can actually work in your favour and mean that you achieve your goal more quickly, or maybe even to a higher standard. Many people shy away from risk-taking because they don't want to risk failing. For example, if you were offered a more senior job with a larger salary in a new company, would you take the risk of moving companies, going through probation and getting established in a new team and a new environment if your current job was secure and stable? Or would you choose to stay where you are, to keep that stability and security? It's the same with if you are considering starting up your own business, many of us get to a point in our lives where we have had enough of the 9-5 job and want to use our skills, creativity, knowledge and motivation to become an entrepreneur. We are surrounded by many females, mums and even students who have become successful entrepreneurs, therefore why can't we? Changing track could be seen as a risk if you are considering giving up a stable consistent job to branch off on your own. You would need to consider the funding, your own income, work space, the impact on your lifestyle and those who are dependent on you. However, this could be the best decision you make to take this risk in order to reach your goals and become successful in what you really love doing.

I remember setting up my business at a time when I was quite vulnerable. I was going through a separation and buying my own property whilst also trying to continue in my full-time career and be the best mum I possibly could. All my money was tied up in buying my own property, my time was spent working 12 hours a day and also I was trying to be a good mum. But I knew what I wanted to achieve, and I knew that if I didn't take the risk of investing in myself and in this opportunity, I would never know if it would be a success or not. I struggled for financially for months, because I took the risk of investing everything I had into a new business. It meant that life wasn't as easy as it had previously been, I found that I was spending every spare minute I had on my new business trying to set it up and create a brand / community. I felt like I was failing as a mum and as a business owner because I couldn't work out how I could do everything and therefore wasn't doing anything effectively. But I didn't give up. I kept powering on through and keeping a positive growth mindset. I continued having sleepless nights, financially hard months and exhausting long days because I KNEW I HAD TO MAKE THIS WORK. My daughter was my motivation. I wanted to live a life where I felt I could provide for her, spend more time with her and make her proud of what I had achieved. I faced many challenges along the way and had to take on new risks that petrified me, but if I hadn't have done that, I wouldn't be where I am today.

If you take risks, you are likely to make more mistakes than non-risk-takers. However, as mentioned earlier, you can then learn from these mistakes, grow from them, and move forward towards your goal. People who make mistakes are generally those who succeed – but this may take some time and they may make many mistakes in the process. If you see failing as a step forward, you are bound to succeed, because you use mistakes as opportunities to learn.

How can you learn from your mistakes?

If you are open to learning and growing, your mistakes could be the most important parts of your progress to achieving your end goals. I suggest following this three-step process to learn from your mistakes and move forward.

1. **Acknowledge your mistake.** Realise that you have made a mistake in the first place. Sometimes it is hard for us to own up to a mistake, especially if it affects other people. But the challenge here is to acknowledge the mistake you

have made and the outcome of that mistake. You should also recognise that your mistake is an opportunity to improve. Understand what happened and fully accept that it went wrong.
2. **Reflect.** Reflect on your mistake and ask yourself: What went wrong? Why did it go wrong? What could I have done differently or changed to prevent the mistake happening in the first place? Reflection is key to moving forward. Until you have reflected on your mistake, you will not be able to understand the reasons for it and its impact. While reflecting, also think about why you don't want to make this mistake again.
3. **Plan.** Formulate a plan for how to avoid the mistake happening again. Many people make a mistake then, a few days later, make the same mistake because they have not reflected on the process or made a plan for moving forward. If you have a plan to avoid making the mistake again, then you will be able to move forward. Ideally, be flexible with your plan but include detail.

Limiting Beliefs

Failure and making mistakes are fears that many people have - this is also known as a limiting belief. Limiting beliefs are things that are holding people back from achieving their goals and are often fears. They are opinions that you believe are true, but often prevent you from moving forward and growing. They can keep you stuck in a negative state of mind and stop you from reaching any desire. What you believe about yourself and the world around you shapes your reality. It impacts what you do and what you are able to achieve such as being able to reach the goals that you set yourself. When you are hold onto limiting beliefs, they can often impact what you are able to manifest. Limiting beliefs can form in our childhood and be influenced by parents, carers, teachers, friends and many other sources, sometimes we are not even aware of these beliefs.

We need to be able to identify these limiting beliefs so that we can transform them and replace them with beliefs that will help us become more empowered and progress towards achieving our goals.

Here are some examples of limiting beliefs that people often have:

1. I am too old / I am too young
2. I'm not intelligent enough
3. I'm afraid of trying and failing
4. You have to have money to make money
5. I've already tried everything
6. I don't feel that I really deserve it
7. I don't have the willpower
8. All the good ones are taken
9. I can't trust anyone!
10. I'm always unlucky when it comes to success and money.

There are many other limiting beliefs that people can hold on to, and we have to try and let go of these beliefs as they are often at the root of what is stopping us from achieving our goals.

When I was setting up my own business 'Actually, I Can!' I had limiting beliefs and fears about failing, people's judgement and getting into debt with setting up a new business. I would often shy away from the idea of actually launching and feared failure. The 'imposter syndrome' would sometimes kick in and stopped me from progressing forward. However, after adopting a growth mindset and realising that challenges are all part of the entrepreneur journey, I was able to visualise my goal. I knew what I wanted to achieve and knew what I needed to do. I gradually grew my confidence and self-belief and used all resources possible to support me such as having my own coach, daily affirmations, journaling, reflection and reviewing my business plan. Over the months I made progress and was then able to launch my business. This demonstrates the power of a growth mindset and the impact it can have on transforming your limiting beliefs.

There are some simple steps which you should follow to overcome your limiting beliefs:

> **Step 1: Identify your goal and what your limiting belief is** (you have hopefully already done this). What are your desires, goals and dreams and what is holding you back from achieving these? What limiting belief do you have which is attached to these? Think carefully about any fears or concerns you have with moving forward.
>
> **Step 2: Question and challenge your limiting beliefs.** Limiting beliefs are often instilled from our previous memories in our past or can come from other sources. These are ideas or opinions and are not actually real, they may seem real to you but that is your perspective. You need to be able to question your limiting beliefs to really focus on where the belief has come from and challenge why you have it. For example: Is this belief really grounded? What evidence supports this?
>
> **Step 3: Consider the consequences of your limiting beliefs.** Consider the consequences attached to your belief, what will happen if you are not able to change this belief? How will not changing this affect your life? How will this make you feel?
>
> **Step 4: Choose a new positive and empowering belief.** You must now choose a new empowering belief to adopt that you

would like to use moving forward and how you will apply this. Ensure that this new belief is believable for you and will support you in moving forward. What new belief do you want to choose? What are the advantages of this new belief? How will this belief change your life for the better?

Step 5: Consistently apply this new belief to your life daily. Ensure that you now apply this new belief into your life every single day. Find different ways of being able to do this such as: Neuro-Linguistic programming techniques, visualisation or daily affirmations. Find a technique that works for you so that you can daily embed this new belief into your mind and your life.

If you apply these steps to transforming your limiting beliefs, you should be able to move on towards achieving the goals you have set out for yourself.

Now it's your turn

Write down three things that you have failed at or made a mistake in. Were you able to overcome your failure? Did you try again and succeed? If you didn't, then why do you think this is the case?

Formuate a plan for how to avoid making the same mistakes again. What would you do differently?

Write down what your current limiting beliefs are from achieving your goals. How do you think you would be able to overcome these?

Remember that if it was easy everyone would be doing it!

CHAPTER 5

Your Mindset

Our mindset determines our success in life. It can empower us as well as give us confidence and drive when we need it the most, or it can limit us and make us doubt ourselves, stopping us from reaching our goals. Negative thoughts tend to attract negativity. If you believe that you can't do something, then normally you can't.

Do you look for negatives and hold on to them, focusing on them instead of on positives? How can we shift our minds and our thoughts to focus on what we want to happen and the positives in life? Think about a day at work. You arrive home at the end of your day and your partner/parent/other family member asks you how your day was. How often do you talk about the negative things that happened in your day rather than the positive? For example, do you talk about the meeting that didn't go to plan, or the friend who never called or texted you back? Or do you talk about the great work you completed with clients that day or the interesting conversation you had with your manager about a new strategy at work? Your mindset can dramatically affect your health and well-being. If you are regularly focusing on the negative, there is less time for you to focus on the positives, affecting your overall happiness and success.

I often love to apply the mindset to the simple concept of the half full / half empty glass. Is your glass half empty or half full? If your glass is half full, you are conscious that there is room to fill your glass with progress, knowledge, success and everything you wish to aim for. It is the optimistic viewpoint. If your glass is half empty, you are already rejecting the opportunity to fill the glass. Instead you're focusing on how empty the glass is – the pessimistic view. That viewpoint indicates how that person sees situations in life.

As adults we are constantly learning new skills and developing as individuals. We have the opportunity to continue to grow and become the best version of ourselves; however, it is all down to our mindset as to how we approach challenges and working towards our goals in order to achieve the intended outcome. Setting realistic goals and coaching yourself to believe that anything is achievable puts you in charge of your own success. You don't give up after one try; you keep going. Ask yourself questions such as 'Did I succeed? Did I give it enough time? If my first strategy didn't work, what could I change? What feedback can I take on board?' Apply this rule to an athlete – someone who is regularly training to become strong and fitter. Do they get fitter and stronger because of the time and energy they put into their training, or are they becoming fitter and stronger because they believed that they would through a positive mindset? Could it be a combination of the two? Although training regularly and eating a good diet are important to an athlete, with the correct mindset your goals will be easier to achieve. Research shows that 80% of your success is due to your mindset and the other 20% is strategy and all things in between. This demonstrates how important the mindset really is when it comes to working towards your goals and it can have a big impact on the progress you make. This can be applied to any goals that you set yourself in life. Combine mindset work and a clear strategy will give you maximum opportunity of achieving the ideal outcome.

I can talk from experience. When I started writing this book back in January 2020 I was motivated and bursting with ideas. I wanted to share with the world my knowledge of mindset coaching and positive psychology and my views and experiences. However, there were days where I procrastinated, days I had writers block, and days where I allowed my limiting beliefs to creep in which slowed down my progress. Over the 18 months it took to compete the book, I had to consistently work on my mindset as well as my strategy of writing. I was used to working on my mindset regularly anyway, therefore continued with applying various effective mindset techniques such as meditation, affirmations, journal writing and specific mindset exercises as well as working on my writing strategy in order to produce a finished book. This demonstrates that strategy and skill on its own won't always produce the end result that you want to achieve; however, combining strategy with mindset work is more likely to encourage progress, results and achieve the end goal.

Why develop a positive mindset?

Anyone can achieve a positive mindset. It's a mental and emotional attitude that doesn't always come naturally to everyone, but is a habit that you can adopt and develop. You have to train your mind to see the positives in life. This needs work, dedication and focus. Many people find that developing a positive mindset makes them feel happier and more energised. However, not everyone finds it easy to have a positive mindset; some people are naturally more pessimistic than others, and find it hard to be positive when negative things happen to them, or when they are in a negative situation. Being fearful of what we don't want to feel or experience – such as loneliness, not being accepted, failing an exam or interview – is very common, and the fear of failure is something we all experience. It's a skill to train your mind to think positively. A mental utopia, where everything is perfect and how you envisioned them to be, is not easy to visualise. Most people worry about the future and potential problems that may occur. This creates anxiety within us and therefore leads to negative thoughts about what could or might happen – 'what if I get ill? What if my boyfriend leaves me?'

There are a number of benefits to having a positive mindset. These include:

- You are generally **healthier and sleep better.** Because you're not worrying about things and you are thinking positively about your goals, you are able to relax more, which helps you to be more healthy, both mentally and physically. Eliminating stress and anxiety will help you to sleep better, and you will generally feel more energised and healthy.
- You develop **better well-being, both mentally and physically**. Thinking positively improves your mental well-being because you are thinking happy thoughts about your situation and your goals.
- You are generally **happier.** The more positively you view your life, the happier you become and the more you enjoy life.
- You **develop skills** in a range of areas. Positive thinking helps you to develop skills within your profession, and you learn more easily because you believe you can. You are also better able to learn skills from others, since your positive mindset prompts you to learn new things.
- You **develop more self-confidence.** The more you believe you can achieve the goals you set for yourself, the more your confidence will grow. Confidence is a hard attribute to develop if you do not think positively.

- You generally **have lower levels of depression and stress.** This is because you're always thinking positively.
- You are **more resilient.** You increase your ability to cope with problems and to continue working towards your goals, regardless of any hurdles that you may face on the way.
- You have **more energy.** You create energy through positive thinking, and this motivates you to want to achieve. The more energy you have, the more likely you are to continue working towards your goals.
- You **feel stronger.** Because you have more energy and a positive outlook on life, you will naturally feel stronger and more powerful. This strength will give you the boost you need to continue working towards your end goal.
- You are **more successful.** With more energy, resilience and confidence, you are able to work harder towards your goals.

By having a positive mindset and believing you can achieve what you are trying to achieve, you are more motivated, persistent and determined, which are all key ingredients to succeeding in anything. A positive mindset also cultivates self-confidence and self-esteem.

Take me as an example. When I started exploring the possibilities of starting my own business 'Actually, I Can!' I had many fears about failing, people's judgement and falling into debt with setting up a new business. However, I tried to remain positive throughout the entire process and immersed myself in the feeling that anything I plan and want to achieve is possible. As mentioned previously, my limiting beliefs would creep in every now and then. Though mindset work I was able to overcome these and push through them. Overtime, I developed the knowledge and skills over time about setting up a business and I felt motivated and positive. As I gradually moved towards my goal of launching the business, I was energised every day.

I developed more confidence over time as I grew to know and love my brand, my vision and my aims of the business as well as building my own resilience and preparing for whatever came my way. Over time, I saw the progress I was making and the opportunities that were created in order to achieve my goal of launching a successful business. If it wasn't for the resilience and positive mindset, my business may not have existed today and therefore I may have never been able to help and support other women with their mindset and goals in order to create the best version of themselves.

The qualities listed below will help you to develop a positive mindset so that you can achieve your goals:

- **Gratitude.** Be grateful for everything you currently have in your life, even the smallest things. Also, share your gratitude with others through acts of kindness and saying thank you.
- **Accept failure and learn from it.** Accept that you will not always be successful, especially with your first attempts, and consider what you can learn when things don't go your way.
- **Optimism.** Always be optimistic: approach everything with an optimistic mind, thinking that anything is possible. Then you will be able to achieve whatever you have set out to do.
- **Resilience.** Be determined to succeed. Never give up. Keep on trying if at first you do not succeed. It's important to be motivated to continue trying and to be persistent with your aims and goals.
- **Criticism.** Learn to take criticism positively, and consider what you can change following the criticism. Criticism can be hurtful, if it is not given properly. Criticism should be constructive and specific. The key is learning how to deal with criticism: don't let it set you back in any way.

- **Environment.** Create and live in a positive environment. If you are surrounded by negativity and negative people, you will struggle to be positive yourself, so your environment is a very important factor in creating and developing a positive mindset.

If you combine these qualities and factors and stay away from negative emotions, thoughts and discussions, you are giving yourself the best opportunity to develop a positive mindset. Having a positive mindset makes it more likely that you will achieve any goals and aims you set for yourself.

Being positive is linked to having a growth mindset, where as being negative is linked to a fixed mindset. This concept of growth and fixed mindsets engages with how our mindsets can both encourage us, and discourage us from fulfilling our full potential. Both types of mindset give people two very different ways of viewing life. This table summarises these two types of mindset:

Someone with a fixed mindset	Someone with a growth mindset
Believes that people are born with a fixed level of intelligence	Believes that people can develop their intelligence
Gives up easily	Is resilient and willing to keep trying
Avoids challenges	Embraces challenges
Sees effort as pointless	Sees effort as a journey
Is threatened by the success of others	Is inspired by the success of others
Judges others	Supports others
Sticks to what they know	Likes to try new challenges

Individuals who believe that they can develop and improve through hard work have a growth mindset. These people generally enjoy learning new things and taking on challenges (even if they involve risk), and they value the growth created by these challenges. Having this kind of mindset can help you live a fuller and more meaningful life because you are more willing to try new things, learn from your experiences and believe that you can continue to grow as a person.

Individuals with a fixed mindset do not believe they can learn new skills or improve. They may shy away from challenges because they fear they could fail. This can have a massive impact on their progress and experiences, both at school and at work, as well as in relationships and other aspects of life. Avoiding new opportunities and challenges can prevent people from growing and developing.

The sections below discuss the differences between the mindsets.

Effort and motivation

An individual with a growth mindset believes that effort is an important part of their progress towards their goals. They put in a huge amount of effort over time to achieve the desired result. An individual with a fixed mindset would not put much effort into any task they are set ('What's the point? I'll be no good at it. I've always been rubbish at this') and will have little motivation to complete anything.

Challenge

An individual with a growth mindset loves a new challenge and faces challenges with confidence, drive and motivation. They will not be afraid to fail and will use challenges as opportunities to learn. They are normally excited about trying new challenges. An individual with a fixed mindset tries to avoid challenges and prefers to stay where they are, in their comfort zone, due to their fear of failure.

Mistakes and failing

An individual with a growth mindset doesn't worry about making mistakes. They see mistakes as lessons and can take something positive away from them to continue working towards their end goal. An individual with a fixed mindset will dislike making mistakes and will feel like a failure when they make a mistake. They will often feel embarrassed about their mistakes and may want to cover them up or make them disappear.

If we look at these mindsets, we can see that there is a huge difference between them in relation to outlook on life in general and attitude towards challenges, tasks and goals. The majority of us want to have a growth mindset – or to develop one – to achieve our goals and dreams. If you want to develop a growth mindset, you first need to understand what kind of mindset you currently have. People who already have a growth mindset should think about developing it further to maximise its benefits. If you have a fixed mindset, you should aim to develop a growth mindset.

How do you know if you have a fixed mindset or a growth mindset? Answer the following questions to find out...

1. Are you a positive person?
2. Do you believe that you can achieve your full potential?
3. Do you believe that your intelligence is not fixed and that you can become smarter?
4. Do you believe that hard work and perseverance give results?
5. Can you create opportunities for yourself?
6. Do you love taking on new challenges?

7. Do you believe that you can learn from mistakes and failure?
8. Do you avoid negativity?
9. Do you feel that positive language helps create a positive mind?
10. Do you believe that you can achieve whatever you set out to achieve?

If you answered 'yes' to all of these questions, then you are likely to have a growth mindset. If you answered 'no' to most or all of these questions, then you are likely to have a fixed mindset. Even though most of us will have said 'yes' to at least a few of these questions, we need to think about how we can use this mindset to achieve what we want to achieve. The key here is to treat life, and situations in life, like a staircase. Most staircases have many steps. Imagine that each step of the staircase is taking you one step closer to your goal. You might be tired from climbing, and sometimes the staircase can take ages to ascend, but when you reach the top, whatever is waiting for you at the summit will have been worth working for. You could relate this to climbing a mountain, such as Snowdon in Wales. If you have never climbed a mountain before, or if you haven't trained for it, then you will physically find it harder than those who climb and train regularly. Every step up the mountain, especially the second half, can be a struggle. However, with every step you are getting closer to the top. If you tell yourself that you won't make it, that you can't keep going, these thoughts will impact how you feel physically and how much energy you have to complete the climb. If you tell yourself that you can achieve it, that you will reach the top and that you need to keep going, you will find that you will push yourself harder to keep going. Believing that you can reach the top is very important – and the feeling when you do is unbelievably satisfying.

Here are the growth mindset steps to success. These can be applied to most aims and goals. At the bottom of the steps you will notice that phrases are targeted towards a fixed mindset, but as you climb the steps you will notice that the phrases become more positive and focused on a growth mindset.

Actually, I Can!
GROWTH MINDSET STEPS TO SUCCESS

- I DID IT!
- ALMOST THERE
- MY GOAL IS IN SIGHT
- I KNOW I CAN DO THIS!
- I'M GOING TO DO MY BEST!
- I WILL STAY MOTIVATED
- I AM MAKING PROGRESS
- THIS IS CHALLENGING!
- I'M SCARED OF FAILING!
- I DON'T KNOW WHERE TO START!

I use this concept of 'steps to success' with all of my clients and students in coaching, mentoring and teaching. It is a fantastic way of evaluating how you are feeling about approaching a task or challenge and exploring how you can work your way up the steps in order to achieve the desired outcome. These steps to success can be used on small tasks such as learning a strategy for work / business; or organising your email inbox and diary for the next month, to much bigger tasks and aims such as setting up your own business from scratch. It's a great tool to visit regularly to encourage you to think about your mindset and to address the reasons why you would doubt yourself in achieving your goals, aims or tasks.

Top tips to develop a growth mindset

Here are some top tips to help you develop a growth mindset. If you apply a number of these to your goals, desires and aims, you will soon notice that your outlook is more positive and that you feel more motivated to achieve.

1. **Be brave and confident.** Confidence is extremely important and is valued by many. Have the confidence to set your goals and go for them, never mind how hard they feel or how far away they seem. Be brave on every step of the way up your staircase to success.
2. **Be realistic.** Ensure the goals, aims and tasks you set yourself are actually achievable, not impossible. Although most things in life are 'possible', double-check that your goals are, taking into account all the factors in your life that will impact these.
3. **Be curious.** Curiosity is a characteristic that is linked to learning. Be curious about what you are trying to achieve and about how to achieve it. Research success stories and think about how you will work towards your goals. For example look at how individuals have successfully started a business from scratch with very little budget, or look at how mums have successfully juggled being a parent and working. Curiosity supports us in becoming more open-minded, encouraging us to consider all ways that we can achieve a goal. It makes us more self-aware.
4. **Be inspired by others.** Think about who inspires you and why. Look at their story, life, methods, philosophies,

successes and mindset. How have they become so successful? What can you learn from them? Most people are inspired by others and how they have become successful. Use the experience of others to help you reach your goals.

5. **Take risks and take on new challenges.** Take on new, exciting challenges that will help you to progress towards your end goal. Be a risk-taker. Tackle challenges head-on with confidence and determination.

6. **Accept failure**. Accept that everyone fails at something and that failure is a lesson to be learned. Think about why you failed, how you could improve things, and what you will do to ensure everything else goes more smoothly next time.

7. **Value the process.** Understand that working towards a goal is a process. Most things don't come easily and take a great deal of planning, hard work and effort. Accept that this is part of the process to achieving your end goal.

8. **Acknowledge that growth happens over time.** Growth is not necessarily rapid. This applies to school, careers and relationships. Look at the growth you have achieved up to now – how have you grown and what have you done to achieve this?

9. **Reflect.** Give yourself the opportunity to reflect on your progress and journey. Reflect on your mindset and how you have approached challenges. What have you learned along the way, and how have you developed as an individual over time?

10. **Love what you do.** Be passionate about what you do and what you are working towards. Love the goals you have set yourself and the process you are following to achieve those goals.

Now it's your turn

What type of mindset do you have now? Think about why you have this type of mindset. What can you do to develop a growth mindset?

How could you use the 'Steps to Success' in your daily routine and for working towards your aims?

Imagine what you can achieve when you stop doubting yourself.

CHAPTER 6

Motivation

Motivation plays a big part towards success. The more motivated we are, the more we are encouraged to do well. When we are motivated, we work hard towards our goals until we achieve them and are happy with the end result. A good example of this is getting fit or losing weight. Many people set themselves goals for losing weight or changing their body shape. If they motivate themselves and use other sources of motivation and support such as personal trainers, fitness influencers' inspiration on social media, fitness programmes, dieting apps and companies or by tracking/monitoring their progress – they are more likely to see progress than someone who is less motivated and who doesn't have the sources of support and motivation. Once they have reached their goal, some people even set themselves a new goal: they are motivated by their success and use their high level of motivation to progress further.

Let's relate this to your work. Are you the sort of person who always arrives on time to work or to online meetings? Do you create a 'to do' list each day that you would like to achieve? Do you set yourself a certain time to complete tasks or jobs, and ensure that it is completed to the best of your ability? Do you strive to succeed, progress and develop as an individual? These are all examples of how people show their motivation, dedication and positivity to their work or job. But how do you ensure you stay motivated?

How can you get motivated – and stay motivated?

We all have things that motivate us in order to complete tasks or challenges; however, sometimes we lack motivation due to various circumstances such as lack of interest, lack of energy or lack of knowledge. Avoiding the task or challenge will not help you to progress, therefore we need to be able to work out what motivates us the most and what inspires us to want to do well. The three most common answers to this are:

1. Sense of achievement
2. Money
3. Progress/promotion.

Sense of achievement. Many people want to achieve the main goal or aim they have set and are happy with this as an end result. This could be your monthly sales target, formulating a new marketing strategy, or reaching out to 30 new potential clients. Whatever the goal is, achieving this goal really motivates people, especially if your hard work and achievement are recognised by others.

Money. A motivation tool for many people in all kinds of businesses. Many jobs are target-driven, which is attached to bonus schemes, pay increases or incentives. Bonuses can help with personal finances, investments such as homes, and luxuries such as holidays, therefore most people are more than happy to receive a financial gain for achieving a goal.

Progress/promotion. A motivational tool used by many people who want to better themselves. If you have a growth mindset, and know you can develop your skills and knowledge, you will want to do well at work. These people will be motivated to work hard at work to be promoted or to gain new responsibilities.

Developing motivation can sometimes be tricky, especially if you are trying to self-motivate and are not relying on other people to motivate you. Finding ways to increase your motivation can have a huge positive impact on your performance. This is all linked to having a growth mindset – if you believe you can do something, then motivating yourself to work towards it will help you achieve your goal. Becoming more motivated can help you to change your behaviour and attitude towards something, to view an outcome as being more achievable. It can also help to boost your engagement with something which you previously may well have found less interesting or less achievable previously.

So how do you keep motivated when working towards your goals? Well, one of the best ways to work out what makes you tick, what spurs you on and encourages you. Is it money, is it making people happy, it is it a sense of achievement? Everyone's answer to this will be different, but it is a great way to increase your motivation.

There are two types of motivators: intrinsic (what you want to do) and extrinsic (what you have to do). These will encourage you to think in slightly different ways about how you will achieve your goal. Once you have established what motivates you, then you can use this as a tool to support you with completing tasks and challenges.

Simplifying your goals and vision is another way of self-motivation. Think about your goals and how you intend to achieve them. If you are struggling to motivate yourself to work towards those goals, then what can you do to simplify them? Focusing on one or two aspects can really increase self-motivation. If you have a number of goals you wish to achieve and are trying to work on them all at the same time, you may be trying to do too much, especially on top of everyday life. So, look at your goals and see which are most important to you. You may find it more efficient to work on one goal first, especially if it's a long-term goal that will take a long time and focus to ensure that you succeed.

When I started creating my business of 'Actually, I Can!' I was also working full time as an Assistant Headteacher in a school as well as being a mum. I therefore had limited time to spend on planning and developing my ideas for the business. When I got home from work, I would spend time with my daughter, therefore by the time she was in bed I was shattered and lacked motivation to do anything let alone start building a business. I have always been a very positive person; however, my tiredness was limiting my motivation to continue working in the evenings. I then started to set myself small goals (referring back to chapter 2) and managed my spare time carefully. I found that attending coaching sessions in the evenings once a week was very beneficial to my motivation and I would always walk away energised and motivated. I watched a number of inspirational videos on YouTube that helped to focus my mind on my goals and achieving my successes. I discovered a range of podcasts and books that focused on business building and found that listening or reading parts of these helped me to become more motivated. By this time I was in a routine and was able to start building my business from scratch in the evenings and at certain points during the weekend that didn't affect my full time job or being a mum.

Surrounding yourself with positive, motivated people is another way of encouraging you to stay motivated. If you surround yourself with negative people, you will find that your motivation can deteriorate due to their influence. It's amazing how much other people can influence us, both negatively and positively. This doesn't just have to be face to face; our experiences online with social media and messaging can affect us negatively too. Although you cannot choose the people you work with or the mood that others are in, you can try to avoid generally negative people as well as ensuring that you ignore any negative comments so you keep motivated and focused on your own goals.

The internet is a huge part of most people's lives today, but please unfollow, delete, ignore and hide people's stories, posts and comments if they are discouraging you or criticising what you are trying to achieve. On the other hand, there are many people online who influence their followers in a positive way, and you can use these people to motivate you to work towards your goals.

This is a lesson I learnt very quickly in life; negative people create negative energy which isn't good for you. In my teens and early twenties I used to always want to be friends with everyone, to like everyone and for everyone to like me. I always arranged social events and invited everyone in my social circle. Although I was trying to bring people together socially and wanted everyone to be happy and to enjoy themselves, some of those people didn't get on with one another which created friction within the groups. As a result, this created negative energy and issues with friendships. This negative energy wasn't good to surround myself with and therefore I started focusing on socialising with the people who were positive and whose company I enjoyed.

Another strategy to help you motivate yourself is to ensure that, no matter what hurdles you face and what mistakes you make, you always grow through these. An example might be a female business owner not signing any new clients in a month or selling any products. She may feel deflated and upset, however she could use this as a way to research into the reasons why and to adapt and plan to improve for the following month. Or someone being made redundant and having to apply to a number of jobs elsewhere trying to secure another one in the same industry. Never be defeated by hurdles or setbacks. Ensure that you continue learning through your experiences, which will help to motivate you.

We discussed failure in Chapter 4, but this is a perfect opportunity to recap the importance of hurdles and failing from time to time, so you realise that everyone fails from time to time and everyone can recover from setbacks. You must accept that any failures and hurdles that you come across on your journey may be there for a reason: to make you stronger; to help you grow as an individual, and to help you progress towards your goal.

Imagine you apply for a new job. You apply because you felt that you were suitable for the role. You are then told that you don't have the right qualifications and are not the right 'fit' for the company. When you hear this you may feel deflated, upset, perhaps angry or annoyed. However, use this as a lesson: think about how you can make your next application even stronger. Question the company: why were you unsuccessful? What would have made your application stronger? Then work on your application and on your mindset to ensure you're ready for the next opportunity that comes your way.

Another great way to self-motivate is by getting into the habit of doing something, and repeating this habit. This encourages you to continue to work towards the goal. Going to the gym could be an example. Many people join a gym in January following an over-indulgent Christmas, to get into shape for summer. However, statistically the percentage of people who continue to go to the gym a month or two later always dramatically decreases. But if you decide you will go to the gym every Tuesday and Friday morning, you are encouraging your mind to become familiar with this habit and this will motivate you to attend the gym. This can also be applied to mundane chores such as doing the washing and ironing every

Sunday morning. I always used to delay doing the ironing because I couldn't think of anything worse than that. However, I started to make myself complete the ironing every Sunday morning, then, once it was done, I would have the rest of the day free to enjoy quality family time or to work on the career goals I had created for myself.

Increasing your physical and mental energy can also have a big impact on your motivation. Eating a balanced diet and getting enough sleep each night can give you more energy to complete your tasks and goals. If you feel lethargic and tired, this will stop you from feeling motivated. Think back to something you achieved in the past. Were your energy levels high? When we are excited about things, our energy level increases.

Don't compare yourself to others. Our natural instinct when working towards a goal is to compare our progress with that made by our friends, family, competitors and co-workers. The problem with this is that everyone is different with different skills, energy and mindsets. There is no one else like you! When we compare ourselves to others, it can seem like a competition, and it can make us depressed or deflated. Seeing someone else succeed at something you really want or that you are struggling to achieve can affect your motivation and can encourage you to give up, even though there is no reason why you can't also achieve the same outcome. Focus on your own progress. Look at where you were three months ago and where you are now. You will soon see how much progress you have made and how far you have come.

Instead, see people who have achieved what you want to achieve as heroes that you can emulate. You want to join them at the top of the staircase. Look at how they have achieved the same goal or their own goals: study their mindset and the process and strategies they used. What have they done that you could try as a step towards achieving your goal?

I am inspired by other working mums who started up their own businesses whilst raising a family and holding down a full-time job. I followed successful entrepreneurs on social media and very often their posts, stories and examples inspired me to want to succeed and work hard on my own goals. I was also inspired by those around me who worked hard, celebrated their success, and were proud of what they had achieved. In the early days of my teaching career I was always surrounded by enthusiastic, experienced teachers, strong leadership teams and an inspiring headteacher. I used to wonder sometimes how they had so much energy and whether I would ever become that successful. They always used to inspire me and make me feel motivated to work hard and support our students to ensure they achieved their targets and moved towards the career paths they wanted. Over time, I became an Assistant Headteacher on my school's senior leadership team. This was a fantastic achievement and one of which I am very proud.

Make each day count. On your journey towards achieving your goals, think about the journey you are on, think about the steps you have already climbed and the hurdles/barriers you have overcome. Each day you work on your goal means you're a step closer to success. Use this to motivate you by reflecting on where you are now and where you started from.

The benefits of self-motivation

It gives you vision. Self-motivation encourages us to think hard about our end goal. Be clear about what it will look like when achieved. Although our vision of our end goal may be slightly blurry or all the details may not be there at the start, this can develop over time as we focus on what we really want to achieve.

It encourages positivity. Ignoring people around you who create negativity encourages you to be more positive and open-minded. You embrace challenges and plan how to overcome them.

It gives you strength. It helps you to keep going, to keep striving towards your goal, regardless of the hurdles. It encourages you to stay focused.

It brings out the best 'you'. It encourages you to be a positive person who can achieve – and who will achieve. You will be target-driven and full of positive energy. The best 'you' will always make an appearance when you are happy and focused on what you want to achieve. Your mindset plays a massive part in this and can really help to motivate you, creating the best version of 'you'.

Self-belief also plays a massive part of growth mindset. By believing that 'You' can achieve your goals will support your motivation in achieving your desired outcome. Although some people really struggle with self-confidence, it's amazing how much it affects you. I remember when I started developing my 'Actually, I Can!' business, I started with an idea, a vision to inspire ALL women of all ages to believe in themselves in order to achieve their dreams and goals. Over years of teaching students, coaching adults and developing people's mindsets, I knew exactly what I wanted to achieve and was motivated and driven by my goal of creating a successful business that would help others to also succeed. However, on a number of occasions I would question myself as I feared failure and worried that I wouldn't be able to make it a success. I would regularly pick myself back up again, but then the same fear and worry would return. I started to seek advice, guidance and support from my own coach, from my family and friends I questioned if I was doing the right thing and if what I would be offering my clients would be well received and beneficial to them. Through many conversations with people, coaching sessions, watching and listening to a number of podcasts, vlogs and reading a wide range of inspirational books and blogs, I had to shift my mindset of fear and worry to focus on self-belief. I was positive about my idea; I knew what I wanted to achieve, but I just needed that confidence to believe that I could achieve this goal of mine. Thankfully, I listened to my intuitions and followed my instinct. Here I am now telling you my story about my previous lack of self-belief.

Now it's your turn

What motivates you? Is it one of the three most common factors listed in this chapter (a sense of achievement, money, progress/promotion)? Or is it something else? Write it down.

Once you have written down what motivates you, think about ways you can stay motivated. What will help? Write these down.

Be the women who became unstoppable.

CHAPTER 7

The Language We Use

'Yes I can!' is a phrase that we probably don't say to ourselves often enough. Interestingly, the language we use – both relating to ourselves and to other people – has a massive impact on how we visualise, and perhaps even reach, our goal. Even with a small task, such as putting together Ikea flat-pack furniture, we can sometimes feel as if the task is never-ending, tricky and intense. However, if we regularly use positive language, we are repeatedly telling ourselves that we *can* do something.

Imagine you were facing a personal challenge. Would you tell yourself 'I can't do this!' or would you say 'I'm going to give it a try and do my best'? If we tell ourselves that we cannot do something, the likelihood is that we won't be able to, because our negative thoughts will make us believe that it is impossible or that we cannot achieve what we set out to achieve. Positive language will do the opposite: it will encourage you to believe that you can do it, and will inspire you to try until you achieve your aim.

Let's look at some language that we use regularly. You can see that many words are negative and will therefore have a negative impact on us. Below is a table of negative/fixed mindset words/phrases and how we can change these to encourage positivity and a growth mindset.

Negative/fixed mindset	Positive/growth mindset
This is too hard. I can't do it.	It is meant to be hard, but challenges help me to grow.
I give up.	I will try again. Maybe this time I will succeed.
I will never be able to do that.	Let me think how I can achieve that, and what skills, resources and support I need to do it.
That's good enough.	I want to make this even better.
Plan A didn't work.	I need to come up with a Plan B.
I'll just ask someone else to do it for me.	I need to think about how I can achieve this. Do I need some help from others?
I'm nervous, and worried that I will fail.	If I fail, that's OK. I can learn from this and eventually I will succeed.

By changing the language and phrases we use, we can motivate ourselves to approach daily tasks and challenges in a completely different way. If we constantly use phrases like those in the 'Negative/fixed mindset' column, this will have a corresponding negative impact on how we think about ourselves, and on our ability to complete tasks. An example could be you telling yourself that you will never be able to grow an engaged audience on social media of over 10,000: 'I don't know enough people' or 'I'll never be able to reach an audience of 10,000 because I'm not a celebrity!'

Here, you could change the language you use by thinking: 'I may not know 10,000 people; however, if I create engaging content that will educate, entertain and offer value to people, I will be able to increase my engagement over time.' The same applies to the language you use towards others. When speaking to your family, children, friends or colleagues, if you say that someone will not be able to do something, then this will have a negative impact on their mindset and will affect their ability to perform the task in question. Words are very powerful, and influence people's opinions and mindsets. If, as a young child, you are told by your parents that you will never be able to play the piano because you're not talented enough, you would automatically believe them and feel deflated before you even try. Young children generally believe what they are told by their parents. However, if you believe that something is possible and receive positive language from others, you are more likely to give the challenge a go.

It's so important for leaders to lead positively, and to use language that will inspire and motivate others. After all, who would want to work or learn from someone who is negative, unsupportive and discouraging? The language and words leaders use are important for how others perceive them as a leader. Words can also help to build people in careers and can be the creative change needed for a company or brand. Positive, supportive words can empower people and help them with their tasks. Negative language can disempower people.

The people around us and the language they use has a great impact on us, although it is down to us as to how we interpret other people's words. If we use positive language and we hear positive language around us, we are more likely to believe, achieve and succeed.

Affirmations

Saying daily affirmations is a great way of using positive language to create a growth mindset. Affirmations work with your mind rather like exercise does with the body. If you practise these daily, they will help to eliminate any negative thoughts and will replace these with positive affirmations. Your subconscious will receive these thoughts, and will react accordingly. Affirmations remind yourself of the values you care about and the interests you have.

Here are some of my affirmations that you can use to motivate yourself each day:

> Little girls with dreams become women with a goal & a vision.
>
> Show gratitude for what you have today and see how this builds on your tomorrow.
>
> She stopped saying 'But I can't' and started saying 'Actually, I can!'
>
> A positive mind and a growth mindset is everything!
>
> Visualise what you want to achieve… and make it happen!
>
> 'I see it, I believe it, therefore I CAN achieve it!'
>
> Women are no longer meant to be passive and look pretty – they are meant to be active and live their dreams!
>
> Successful women work hard and succeed on purpose: luck has nothing to do with it.

Surround yourself with people who inspire you to believe in yourself and to reach your goals.

Invest in yourself & create your own success story.

There are different ways to use affirmations. Some people say them out loud before completing a task or challenge they are facing, whilst others prefer to say them quietly to themselves every morning before starting the day. There is no one 'correct' way. Find the way that works best for you. The best time to focus on affirmations is when your mind is in its alpha state, when you are relaxed. This allows you to be more receptive and open to ideas and positive suggestions.

It's also important to use an affirmation that relates to your current situation – so, if you want to develop your confidence, your affirmation could be 'I am confident and worthy, I can achieve my goal!'

To create an affirmation, follow these simple steps.

1. Think about the elements in your life that are negative or that you find challenging.
2. Turn these negatives into positives by creating an affirmation statement. It should be believable, specific and brief.
3. Regularly repeat this affirmation to yourself whenever is most convenient for you – for example, when you wake up in the morning.
4. Reflect on your thoughts at the end of each day to see whether the affirmation is having an impact. (It may take some time before you can see an effect.)

Now it's your turn

Choose three affirmations from the list above. Choose ones that you can relate to. Or you might prefer to create your own affirmations, following the steps above.

Focus on these three affirmations over the next few weeks, then evaluate the positive impact they have had on your mindset.

She stopped saying 'but I can't' & started saying 'actually, I can'

CHAPTER 8

Visualisation

Have you ever visualised something you really want, and hours, days, weeks or years down the line you have gained or achieved that exact thing? Is it actually possible to close your eyes and dream of achieving something, and then to achieve it? The Law of Attraction states that if you can visualise something and believe it, you can achieve/receive it.

There is much speculation around whether this is true, especially when it comes to people visualising things such as money. However, I am a firm believer that if you really want something, and you work hard for it, you *can* achieve it. There are no limits to what you can achieve. If you spend some time visualising what you want, your mind will automatically then focus on this. We all know that focusing on something enough, believing in yourself and putting in lots of hard work usually pays off.

How to use visualisation as a tool

Psychologists have been using visualisation for many years as a tool to support people to motivate themselves, to enhance their performance at work or in a sport, and to help them create the mindset that will help them to achieve their aim. This can be so effective that a musician, for example, could visualise a piece of music and visualise playing it on the piano without actually playing it. The mind is such a powerful tool: we as humans have full control over what we see, how we feel and therefore how we act. Our brains are constantly visualising future experiences through our subconscious. These experiences are often influenced by people around us and factors such as TV and social media. However, it is important to focus our minds on challenging these visual thoughts to achieve the outcome we want.

Visualisation does three things:

1. It encourages positive thinking and promotes happy outcomes by encouraging you to visualise your end goal. What will it look like? How will you know when you have achieved it? Visualising your end goal makes it seem achievable and realistic.
2. Because we can see our end goal, we believe it exists or can exist in our lives, which makes us to want to achieve it. This can help us to decide on the best strategies to use to work towards the goal.
3. It helps us to understand what resources we need to be successful and to achieve our goal. This may include tools, strategies, and sometimes even actual materials.</>

I remember being told about visualisation and how it can work if you want something badly enough. OK, I thought, let's give it a go. One evening I closed my eyes and visualised living in my dream home. At first I wasn't too sure how it would work: I was twenty-two, recently out of university, living at home with my parents, and not in a financial position to buy anything like my dream home. But I knew what I wanted to achieve. I realised that if I wanted to achieve my dream home, I wasn't going to be given the money to buy it, or be lucky enough to win the lottery. I knew I had to work for it. Day after day I visualised my dream home. I thought about the furniture I'd buy and the colours I'd paint the walls. At work, I focused on being successful in my career, and I knew this would lead to financial gains over time.

My visualisation didn't just miraculously appear, nor was it given to me like a wish made to a genie. I bought my first house at the age of twenty-three. It was a beautiful house, but it wasn't my dream house. I continued to visualise my dream house for years; I wasn't giving up on this goal. I was doing well at work and, over the years, progressed and was promoted. When I was twenty-seven, I was browsing Rightmove one day and I came across my dream house – the house I had been visualising for years. Could I afford to buy it? Would my current house sell in time for me to buy this house? Was it the right decision? I went to view the house and was in awe of how beautiful it was, and how perfect it was for me. I reserved that house and bought it, which I felt was a great accomplishment, and one I am still very proud of.

Visualisation works both ways, though. Many of us visualise things that we don't want or that we are not looking forward to. In fact, we actually spend more time visualising negative situations and outcomes rather than positive ones. We have a tendency to mull over bad things that have happened to us and replay them with a better outcome for us – 'if only I'd said this in an argument, or if only I'd come up with a smart reply'. We replay them over and over in our minds. This stops us from focusing on our goals; we start to worry about what *could* be and what *might* happen rather that what we can do to make positive things happen. If you have any doubts about a goal or aim, try to let them go, because any negative visualisations can affect the final outcome.

So how can you make visualisation work for you? Think about something you really want to achieve, whether it is your dream job, hitting consistent sales months in your business, or owning a sports car. Visualise that dream or goal. It's very unlikely to happen overnight, and it would be very rare if it just 'happened' or was just given to you. However, if we train our minds to think positively and to regularly visualise our goal/aim, we are encouraging ourselves to have a growth mindset and an optimistic outlook on our lives. Combine this visualisation with the strategies discussed in Chapter 5 as well as positive language, and they will all work together to support progress towards your end goal. We are in control of our thoughts and emotions, and we can control how our mind thinks.

Visualisation may help you to focus on a goal, especially if you are a visual learner. A visual learner is someone who learns through physically seeing things to help them understand what the intended outcome should look like. Once you have visualised what you want, you can start thinking of ways to achieve it. Be as open-minded as you can, and continue to be positive and optimistic. The most effective way of visualising is to focus on what you want to achieve at the end, but also think about how you are going to achieve it, plus all the steps involved. When you visualise, ensure that you are thinking about the details and how the goal/object will look, sound and feel. This will help your brain to formulate strategies to achieve that detailed outcome.

Distractions can be a problem when you're trying to visualise. Find a quiet room. Ensure that everything around you is silent. Put your phone on silent mode or out of sight so that all your focus is on visualising your goal. You can visualise whenever is most convenient for you: you may find that the best time is when you wake up in the morning or before you go to bed at night. Most importantly, choose a time and place that allows you to visualise without any distractions.

Visualisation takes some practice, but is a great technique for those who want to 'see' the end result of their goals, to help them create a pathway to success and think of the strategies they will need to get there. Here are some visualisation techniques that you can try.

Goal/dream visuals (vision boards)

These are actual physical pictures of your goal: for example, your dream house, getting married, having a family or the job title of your ideal job. Having a visual image of what you are trying to achieve can help you to focus on this. Some people have these images by their bed so they see them as soon as they wake up, whereas others create a mood board of their goals. Mood boards are great way to visually display what you would like to achieve. You can include a collage of goals that you intend to focus on at different times in the future.

Affirmations to support goal visuals

As discussed in Chapter 6, creating and repeating affirmations helps to focus the mind. If you combine affirmations with goal visuals, this gives you more detail to help you focus on your goal.

The mental rehearsal technique

This visualisation technique has been around for years and is very effective for athletes. In this technique, the individual closes their eyes and rehearses in their mind the technique they need to perfect or improve, such as taking a penalty, taking off for a long jump, or hurdling. This can be used in many scenarios and situations – such as how to tie a tie or how to braid hair– but mainly relates to skills and techniques rather than knowledge or general achievement.

The visual/audio aid

It has often been said that if you see or hear something often enough, you will remember it and believe it. Think of a catchy radio jingle that you cannot stop thinking about, it is selling a service which you are likely to use, because of the jingle. Or think of a social media ad that is aesthetically pleasing. You are attracted to it, then you remember it and choose to go back to it to and purchase whatever product the company is selling. The same applies to catchy taglines for big brands brand: their slogans are all memorable.

I was once given a A6 poster that said 'see, believe, achieve'. I was encouraged to place this where I would see the poster every day. I placed it on my bedside table so it was the first thing I saw every morning. I found that seeing a positive quote/phrase every morning put me in a positive frame of mind for the day. Another visual aid that has a similar effect is affirmation cards. Use a pack of these when you are feeling low or need a boost, or you could start each day by randomly picking a card and seeing what message it has. You then think about the phrase throughout the day to help you stay positive.

Now it's your turn

Choose the technique you think will work best for you. Try out visualisation, remembering to focus on your goal. Use the growth mindset techniques discussed in Chapter 5 and visualise what you are aiming for in detail. Try doing this regularly and see if visualisation works for you.

Does it help you to achieve any of your goals? Give this a substantial amount of time, then look back.

I see it, I believe it, therefore I can achieve it.

CHAPTER 9

Reflections

When you have adopted a growth mindset and you are approaching situations, events and moments in a different way than perhaps you did before, I think it's important to reflect on the changes you have made and how they have affected you. Starting anything new will always impact on your current practice, and when it comes to mindset it is important to recognise what has changed and how this is positively impacting your life and your goals.

Reflecting can make you more confident about working towards your goals, and can encourage you to be more productive: through it, you learn what you have achieved, what has gone well, and what hasn't, and what you need to do next. Reflecting encourages you to learn from any mistakes you have made and to think about what hasn't worked and how best to move forward. It also gives you perspective, helping you to think about where you are in relation to achieving your goals.

Self-reflection allows us to challenge our thoughts, to consider what we have achieved so far, but also to think about our next steps and to consider all possible outcomes.

An effective way of reflecting on our progress is to keep a reflection journal, where you can write down your goals, your targets and your dreams. I have a reflection journal in which I do this. I revisit my goals and the targets I have set myself every few weeks and evaluate how I am doing. I write down the progress I have made and the impact of the changes I have made. If anything needs to be tweaked I also write this down so that my next steps are clear.

Why use a reflection journal?

1. It allows you to write down your thoughts. In Chapter 2 we explored dreams and goals. It's sensible to start a reflection journal by writing down all your dreams and goals so that you know what your overall goal is and what you want it to look like. You can then start to make plans for how you will achieve this.
2. You can make sense of things that have happened to you by evaluating what has changed since you started working towards your goals and the impact those changes have had. If you seem to be going in the right direction towards your goal, then fantastic! If you're not, then is there anything you can change?
3. It allows you to think about why things are the way they are. Why are things happening to you? This can encourage you to think about the progress you are making and how you can adapt plans if necessary.
4. It helps you plan for future actions based on what has already happened and to think of the next steps you need to take to work towards your goals.</>

There is no right or wrong way to write a reflection journal. Some people prefer to focus on each goal and create a timeline of desired events or an action plan, then evaluate the progress they are making with that. Others prefer to use the journal like a diary and to write daily or weekly entries about how they are feeling, the progress they have made, and what they want to focus on next.

Either way, it's about creating something that will work for you and that you will want to write in on a regular basis. If you start your journal then never revisit it, or don't revisit it regularly, then it may not be the best way for you to reflect.

Another effective way of reflecting on your life is to follow these three simple steps.

1. **What.** Describe what happened, the events that took place, the people involved and any other details.
2. **Interpret.** Consider why those things happened. What impact have they had on your life and the targets you have set yourself? Does this change things? What is the most important event in relation to you working towards your goals? Can the events that have happened be explained? Are they contributing towards you achieving your goals?
3. **Outcome.** Evaluate what you have learned from the day, week or event, then think about what you need to do to adapt or change to ensure that you are making progress towards your goals.</>

The journal you use for your daily, weekly, monthly or regular reflections could be our 'Actually, I can!' reflection journal, which you can purchase online via our website, or it can be a plain notebook. Whatever you decide to use, ensure you set aside time regularly to reflect, so you can assess your progress.

Reflect on where you are now and how far you have come.

CHAPTER 10

The Future

When we think about the future, we might think about how our lives will look and what we will be doing in five or ten years' time. We all want different things, and sometimes the original goals we set ourselves can change. The path we take towards our goals can also alter, depending on life events that happen to us – passing our GCSEs, taking A-levels, having children, getting married, changing career and so on.

> **Whatever you want to achieve in life, it is down to you to aim for it, then achieve it.**

You have the ability to set goals, aim high, think positively, act towards those goals, visualise your end goal and finally achieve that end goal. No one can predict your future; events and challenges will always come about unexpectedly, and you will need to tackle these before you can continue making progress. As you know, you can visualise your goals and set yourself targets, then achieve these by staying motivated and focused.

I hope that the tips and advice I have shared with you in this book will help you to develop a growth mindset, focus on your goals and dreams, and reflect on your journey.

Here are my final ten top tips:

1. Wake up and look at a positive affirmation or read one out to yourself. Remember that positive thoughts and positive language have a major impact on our mindset and that if you regularly look at, as well as read positive affirmations, this will help to motivate you.
2. Remind yourself what you are grateful for and try not to assume that people are either lucky or unlucky. Show gratitude remembering to be grateful for all the positive things in your life.
3. Have a clear plan of your dreams and goals and how you intend to reach them. Make a detailed plan of your goals. Consider short-, mid- and long-term plans, the strategies you will use and the timescales you will give yourself for each one.
4. Visualise what you want to achieve. Ensure you focus on all the details of your end goal and how you want it to fit in your life.
5. Approach hurdles, barriers and challenges with an open mind staying positive, understanding that you will learn from these setbacks. Use challenges and hurdles as lessons: think of ways to overcome these.
6. Regularly reflect on your journey and the progress you are making. Consider the changes you have made, what impact they have had, and what you need to do next to progress towards your goal. Ensure you do this regularly

for the most impact. Using a reflection journal is a great idea.
7. Use positive language all the time; avoid negative words. Remember that the language we use has a massive impact on us as well as on others. Lead by example and use positive language towards others.
8. Share your positivity with the people around you. This is a way of giving, and can change how others view their own life experiences. Share your success stories and strategies with others for them to try themselves to reach their goals.
9. Understand that you won't achieve every goal you set straight away: some goals will be extremely challenging. Accept setbacks and be flexible enough to adapt your strategy appropriately.
10. Believe in yourself. Have the confidence to know, and say, '**Actually, I can!**' achieve the goals I set out to achieve.</>

Your future is full of potential – what it will look like is down to you. With a positive attitude and a growth mindset, anything is possible. We create our own happiness and success by believing in ourselves and reaching for our dreams and goals.

No one else can write your story but you. Follow your excitement, passion and enthusiasm and allow your dreams to come true. Your story is unique to you, so make it one to remember.

Invest in yourself and create your own success story!

Invest in yourself and create your own success story.

ABOUT THE AUTHOR

Kayleigh Greenacre

Kayleigh Greenacre is the founder and CEO of 'Actually…I Can!' which was created to empower and inspire females to believe in themselves and support them with achieving their goals, aims and dreams. She is driven by growth mindset and is passionate about influencing others in order to achieve their full potential. Kayleigh is a firm believer that anyone can achieve their goals providing they apply the right mindset and develop the knowledge and skills in order to do so.

Kayleigh has a background in secondary Education with over 12 years experience and has reached an Assistant Headteacher position. She graduated from Reading University before going into teaching. Whilst developing herself as a teacher, she also completed a Masters

Degree in Education at Bedfordshire University and Post Graduate Certificate in Careers Education at Cambridge University. Since then she has launched the 'Actually, I Can!' business focusing on growth mindset, life coaching and business coaching. She is a certified and accredited Life Coach and Mindset Coach and has continued to develop as a Coach and a motivational speaker, wanting to work closely with females of all ages to support them with their goals and aims both in business and in their lives.

When not focusing on her career, she is at home with her daughter Sofia Grace and other family and friends, enjoying entertaining, playing the piano or saxophone and being creative with film production.

STAY CONNECTED AND GET INVOLVED

I hope I have inspired you to engage with 'Actually…I Can!' and the many opportunities available to you to support with your mindset and self-growth. Visit **WWW.ACTUALLYICAN.CO.UK** and explore the range of programmes and resources available to you. Whether it is one-to-one coaching you are interested in or joining one of our popular leading programmes, there are many opportunities available to you in order to continue developing and growing as an individual. We also have a range of merchandise available online to support you on your journey of developing your mindset and reaching your goals.

Links to website and social media:

Website: **www.actuallyican.co.uk**
Instagram: @kayleigh_greenacre & @actually1can
Facebook: @actually1can
Linked In: Kayleigh-Greenacre
Youtube: Kayleigh Greenacre – Actually, I Can!

Printed in Great Britain
by Amazon